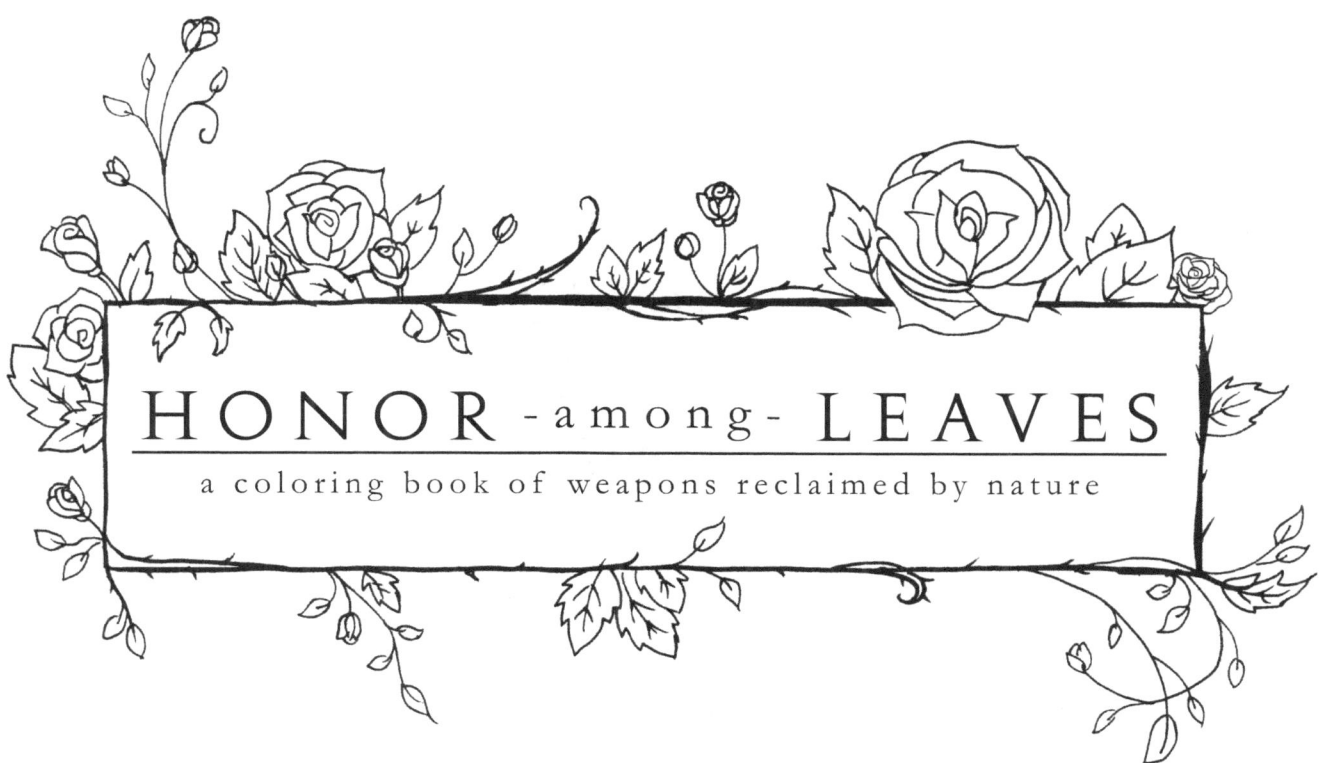

HONOR -among- LEAVES
a coloring book of weapons reclaimed by nature

original hand-drawn artwork by

KARYN SHALDA

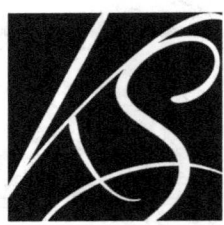

© 2020 Karyn Shalda, all rights reserved.

No part of this book may be reproduced, transmitted, or stored in any form or by any means except for your own personal use or for a book review, without the express written permission of the author:

karyncolors@gmail.com

ISBN 9798578071973

Use this page to test your colors!

Where is the grave of Sir Arthur O'Kellyn?
Where may the grave of that good man be?—
By the side of a spring, on the breast of Helvellyn,
Under the twigs of a young birch tree!
The oak that in summer was sweet to hear,
And rustled its leaves in the fall of the year,
And whistled and roared in the winter alone,
Is gone,—and the birch in its stead is grown.—
The Knight's bones are dust,
And his good sword rust;—
His soul is with the saints, I trust.

THE KNIGHT'S TOMB

- SAMUEL TAYLOR COLERIDGE -

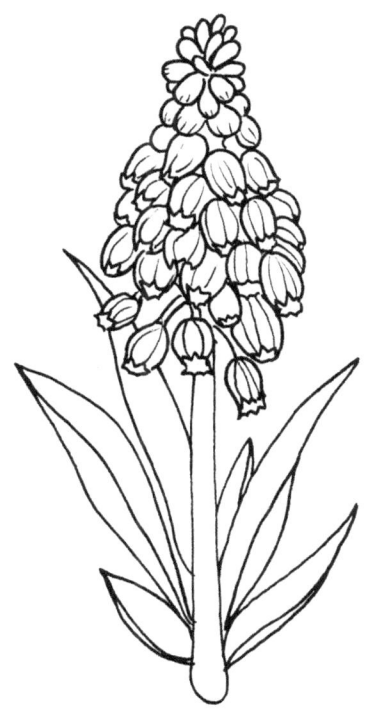

grape hyacinth

BROADSWORD
tulip - lily of the valley - daisy - ivy

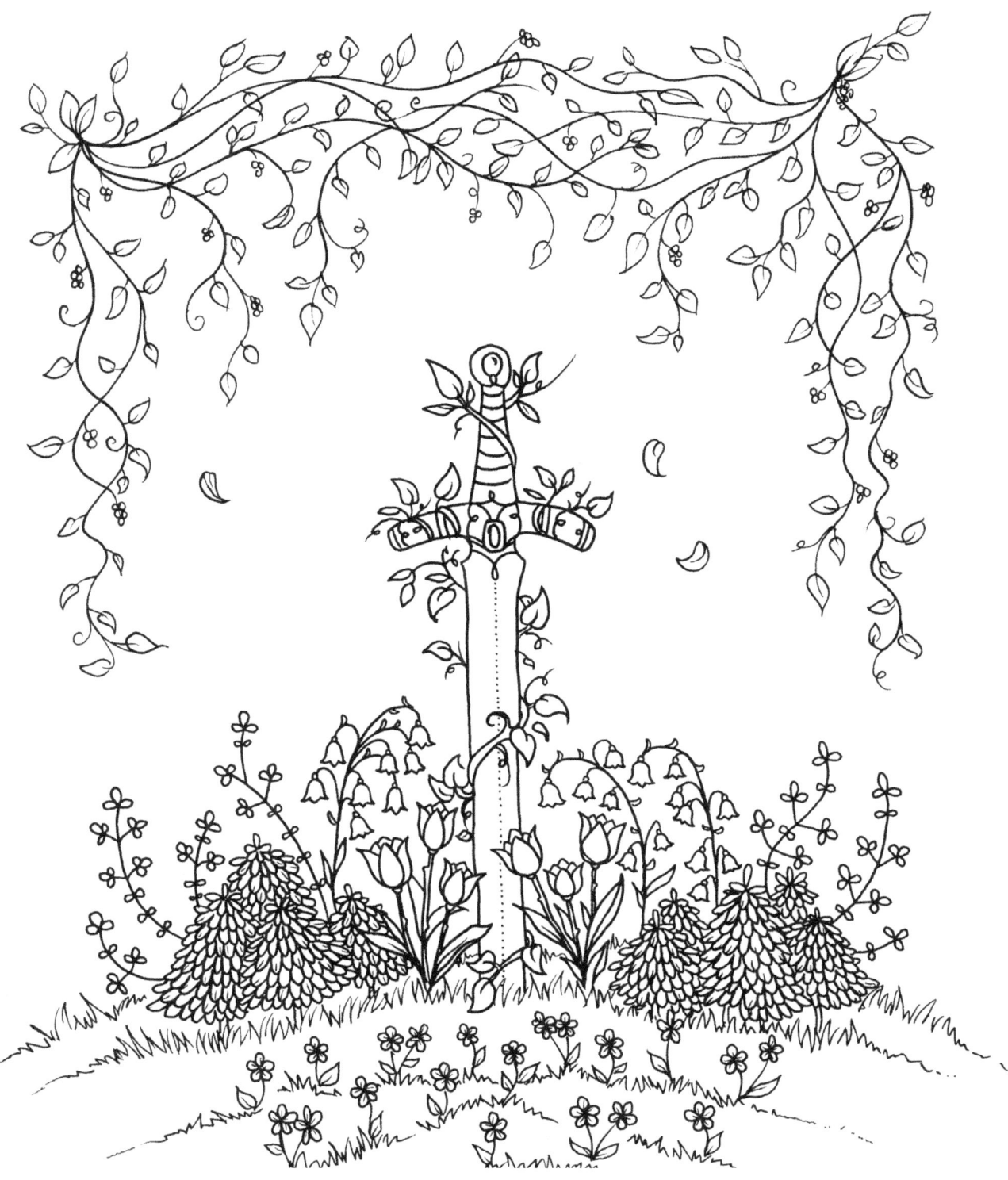

Broad-Axe, shapely, naked, wan!
Head from the mother's bowels drawn!
Wooded flesh and metal bone! limb only one and
lip only one!
Gray-blue leaf by red-heat grown! helve produced
from a little seed sown!
Resting, the grass amid and upon,
To be leaned, and to lean on.

LEAVES OF GRASS

- WALT WHITMAN -

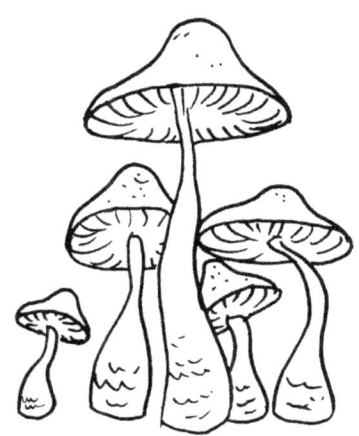

toadstool

BATTLE AXE
mushroom - fern

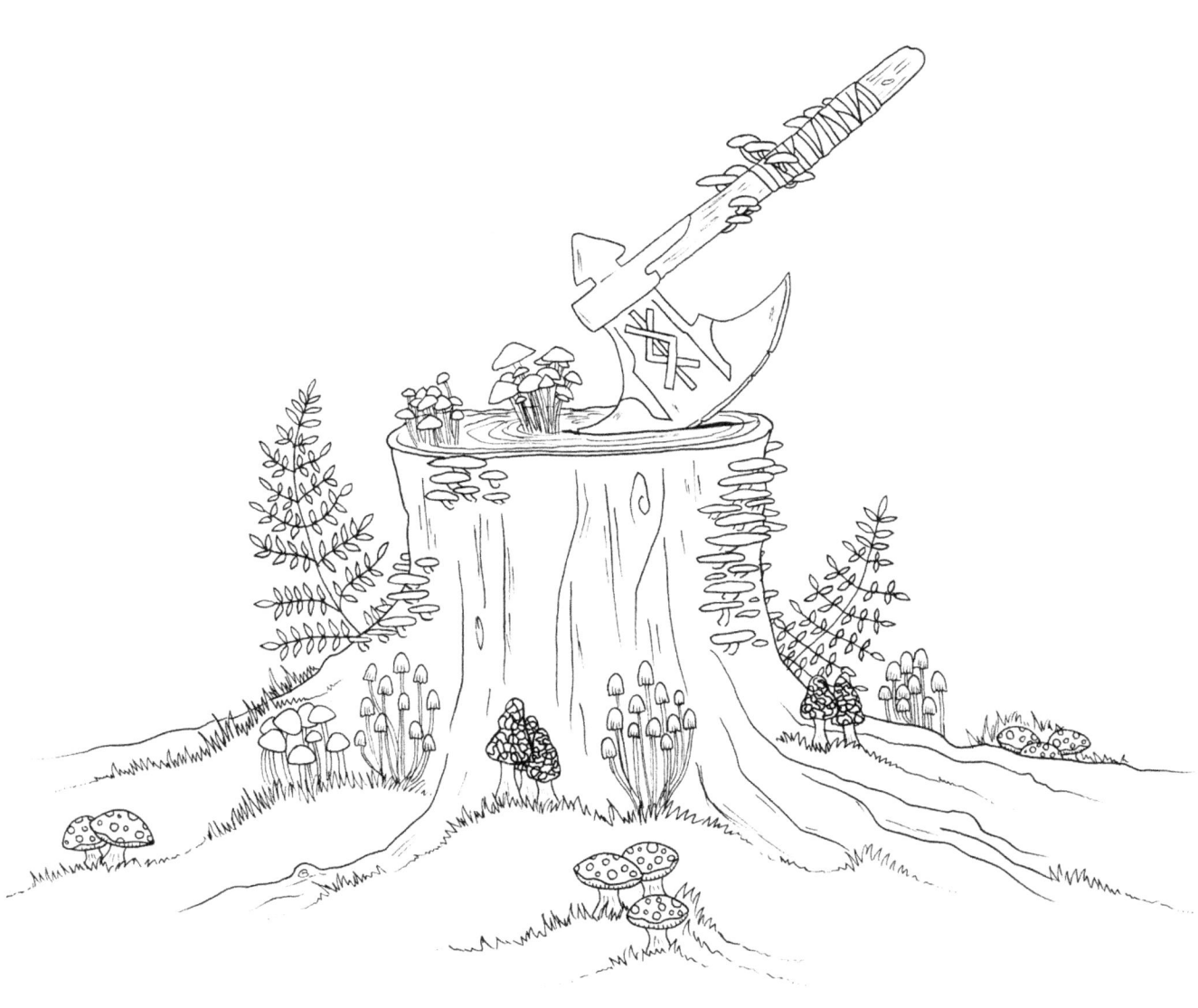

As late I rambled in the happy fields,
What time the skylark shakes the tremulous dew
From his lush clover covert; when anew
Adventurous knights take up their dinted shields;
I saw the sweetest flower wild nature yields,
A fresh-blown musk-rose; 'twas the first that threw
Its sweets upon the summer: graceful it grew
As is the wand that Queen Titania wields.
And, as I feasted on its fragrancy,
I thought the garden-rose it far excelled;
But when, O Wells! thy roses came to me,
My sense with their deliciousness was spelled:
Soft voices had they, that with tender plea
Whispered of peace, and truth, and friendliness unquelled.

TO A FRIEND WHO SENT ME SOME ROSES

- JOHN KEATS -

apple blossom

DAGGERS
strawberry

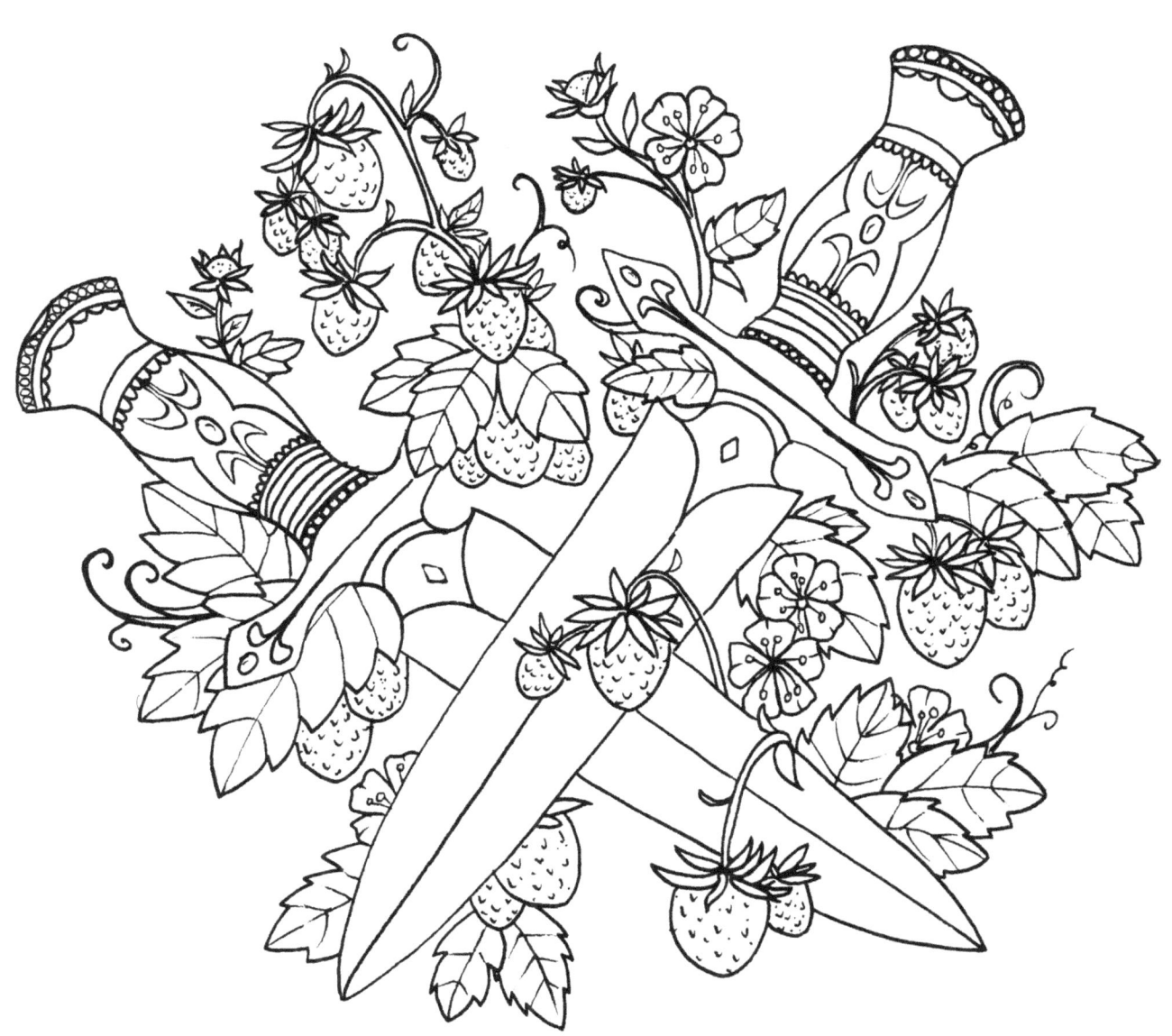

Ah, the noble forms who fought so well
Lie, some unnamed, 'neath the grassy mound;
Heroes, brave heroes, the stories tell,
Silently too, the unmarked mounds,
Tenderly wreath them about with flowers,
Joyously pour out your praises loud;
For every joy beat in these hearts of ours
Is only a drawing us nearer to God.

CHALMETLE

- ALICE RUTH MOORE DUNBAR-NELSON -

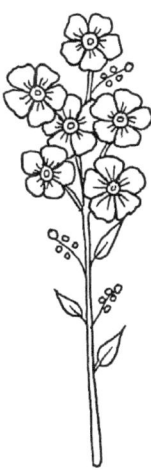

forget-me-not

GLADIUS
bay laurel - gladiolus - narcissus

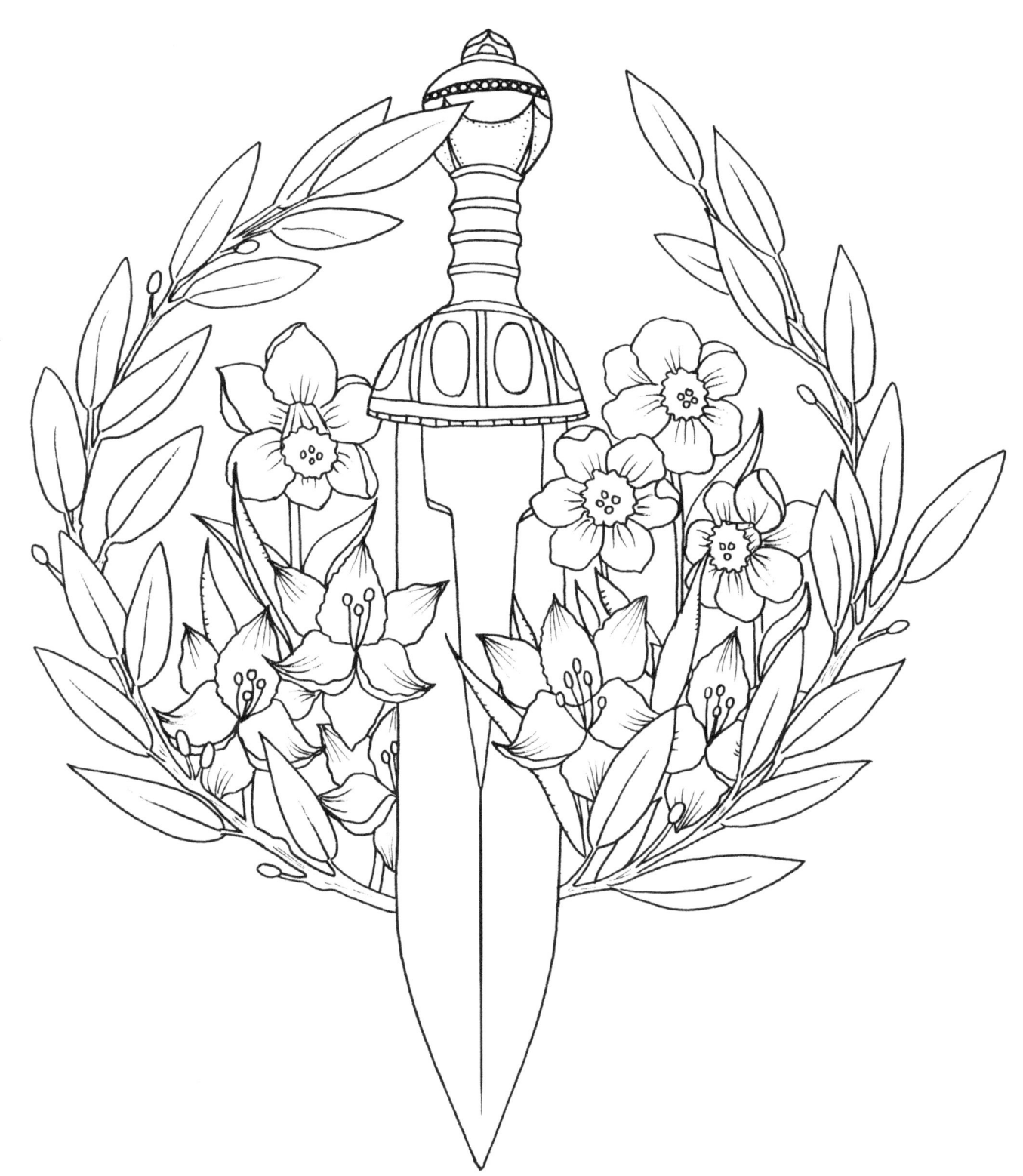

Like trains of cars on tracks of plush
I hear the level bee:
A jar across the flowers goes,
Their velvet masonry

Withstands until the sweet assault
Their chivalry consumes,
While he, victorious, tilts away
To vanquish other blooms.

His feet are shod with gauze,
His helmet is of gold;
His breast, a single onyx
With chrysoprase, inlaid.

His labor is a chant,
His idleness a tune;
Oh, for a bee's experience
Of clovers and of noon!

THE BEE

- EMILY DICKINSON -

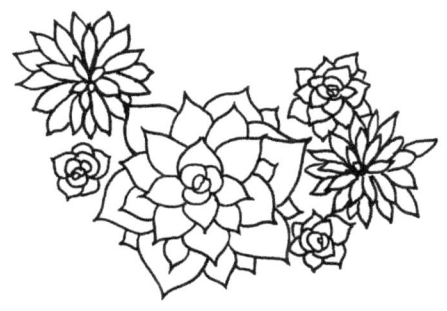

succulent

HALBERD
coneflower - clematis

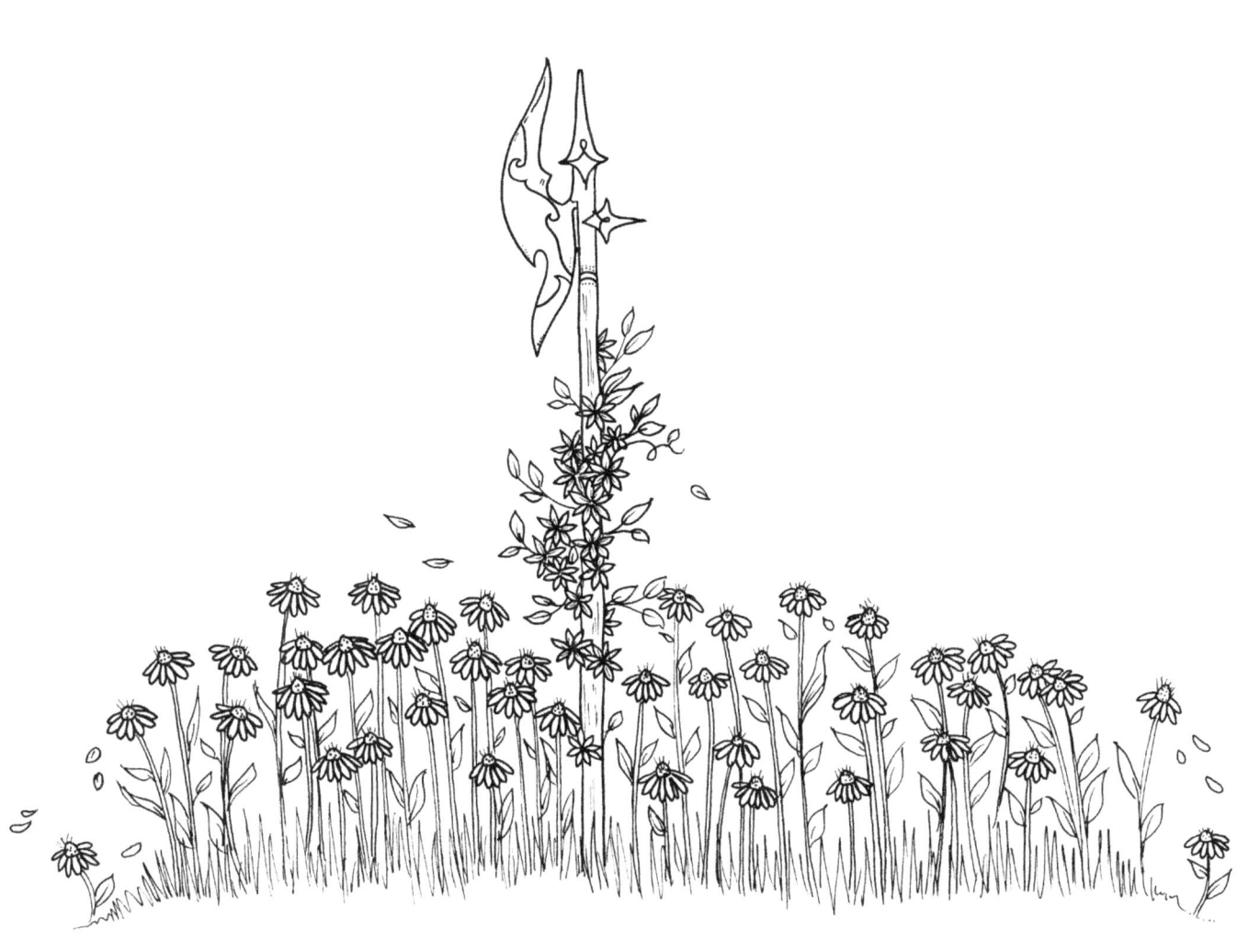

I want to hear the silent sands,
Singing to the moon
Before the Sphinx-still face....

I want to breathe the Lotus flow'r,
Sighing to the stars
With tendrils drinking at the Nile....

HERITAGE

- GWENDOLYN BENNETT -

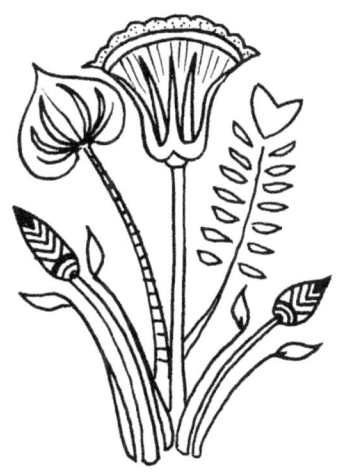

lily - fern - reed

KHOPESH
water lily - reeds - lotus

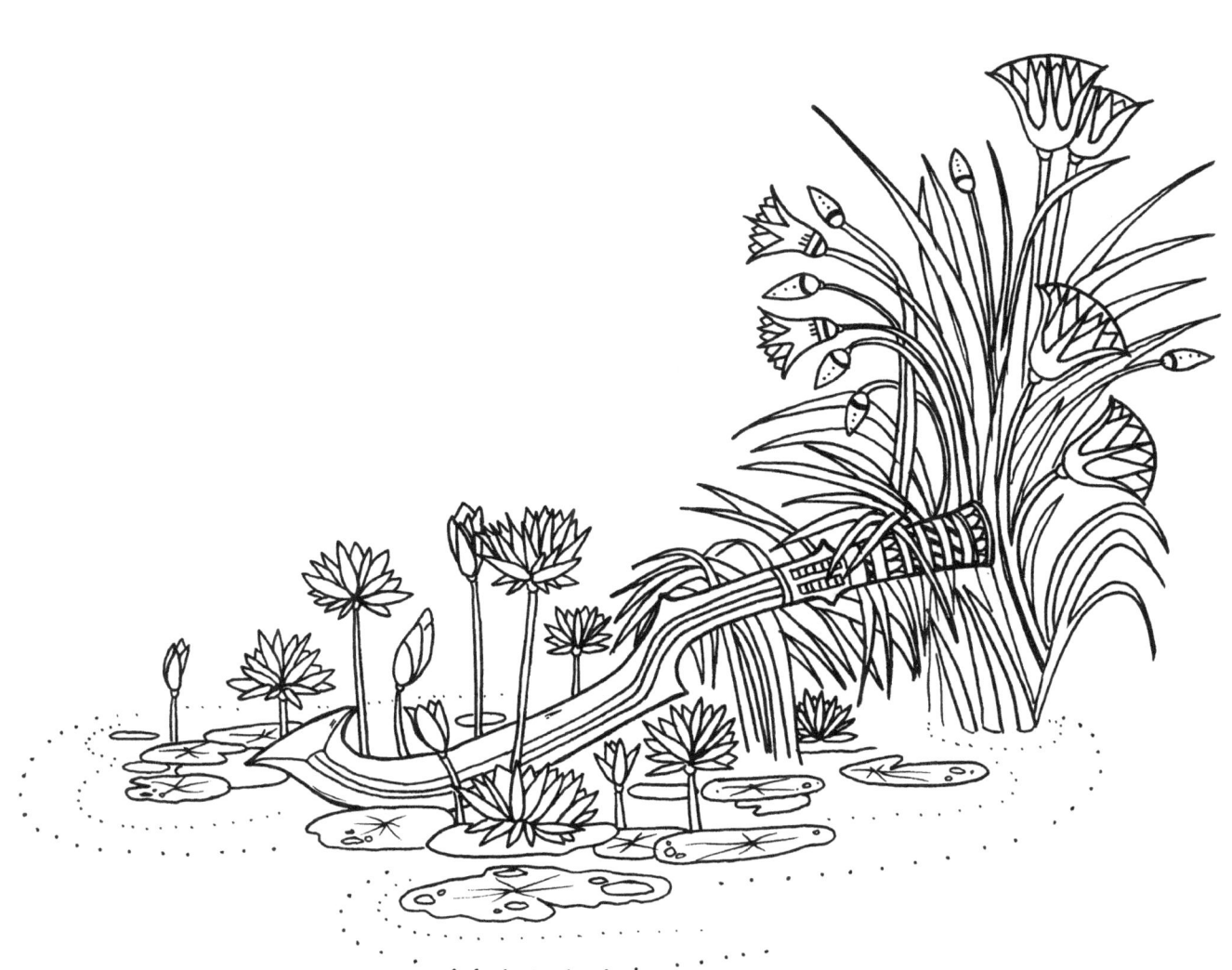

Love came to Flora asking for a flower
That would of flowers be undisputed queen,
The lily and the rose, long, long had been
Rivals for that high honour. Bards of power
Had sung their claims. "The rose can never tower
Like the pale lily with her Juno mien"--
"But is the lily lovelier?" Thus between
Flower-factions rang the strife in Psyche's bower.
"Give me a flower delicious as the rose
And stately as the lily in her pride"--
"But of what colour?"-- "Rose-red," Love first chose,
Then prayed,--"No, lily-white,--or, both provide;"
And Flora gave the lotus, "rose-red" dyed,
And "lily-white,"--the queenliest flower that blows.

SONNET: THE LOTUS

- TORU DUTT -

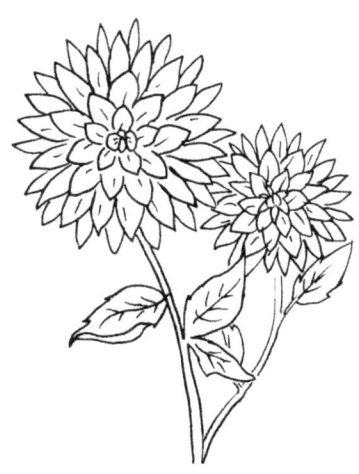

dahlia

KUKRI
lotus

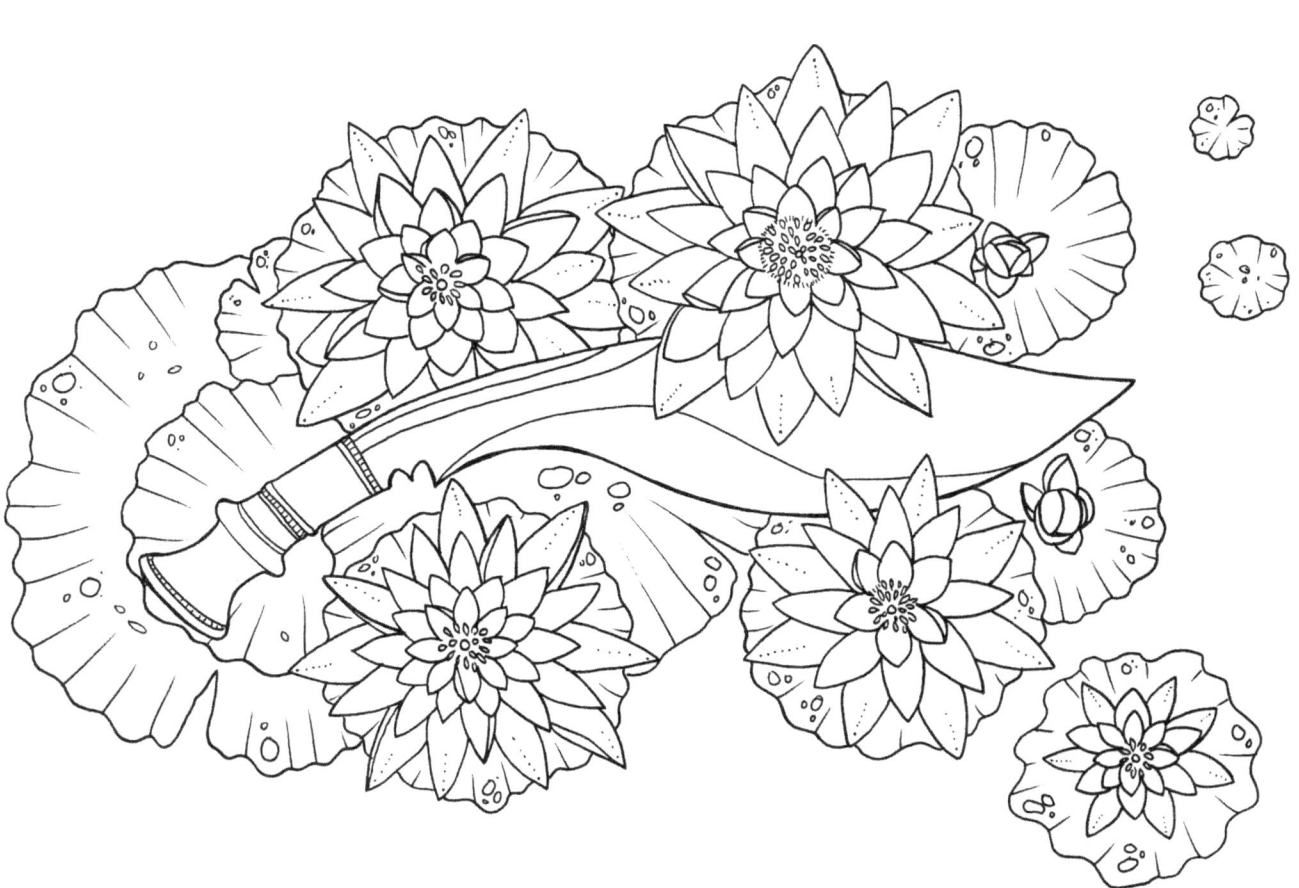

Consider the lilies of the field, how they grow:
they neither toil nor spin, yet I tell you,
even Solomon in all his glory
was not arrayed like one of these.

- MATTHEW 6:34 -

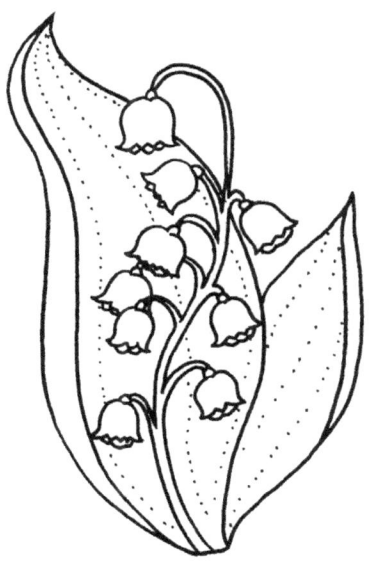

lily of the valley

MORNING STAR
snow drop - christmas rose

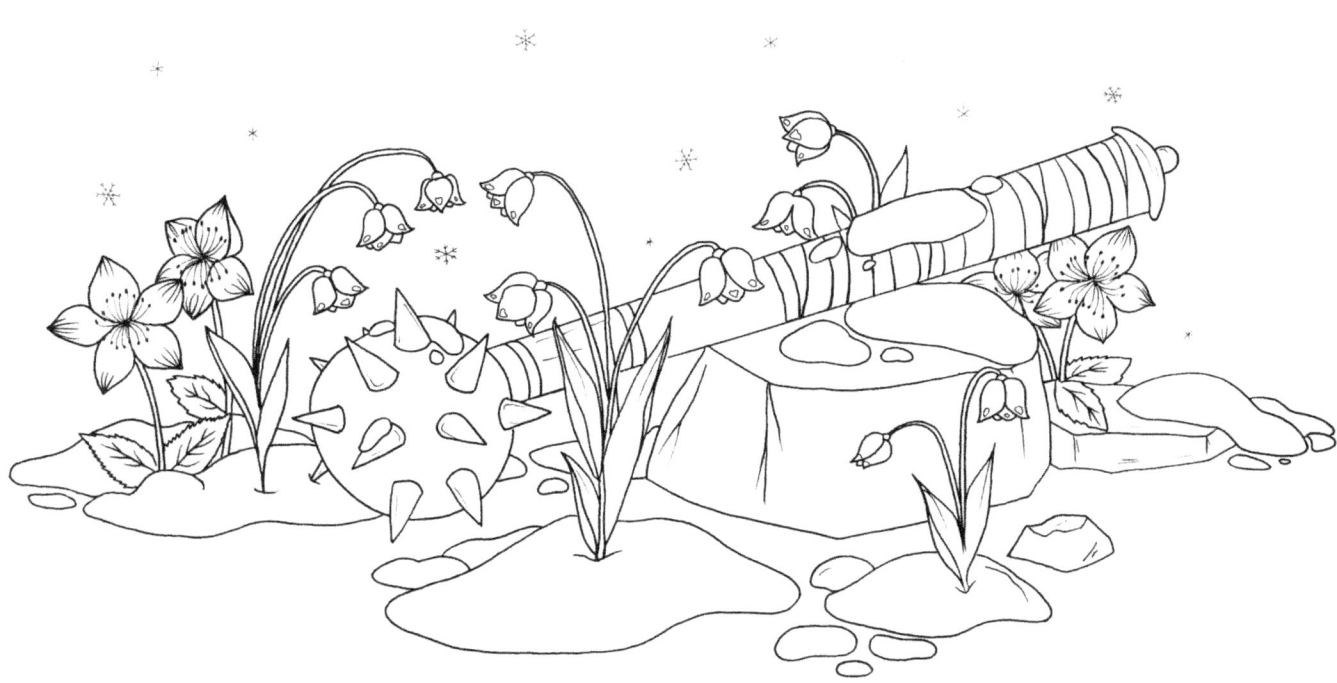

On all her breezes borne,
Earth yields no scents like those;
But he that dares not grasp the thorn
Should never crave the rose.

THE NARROW WAY

- ANNE BRONTË -

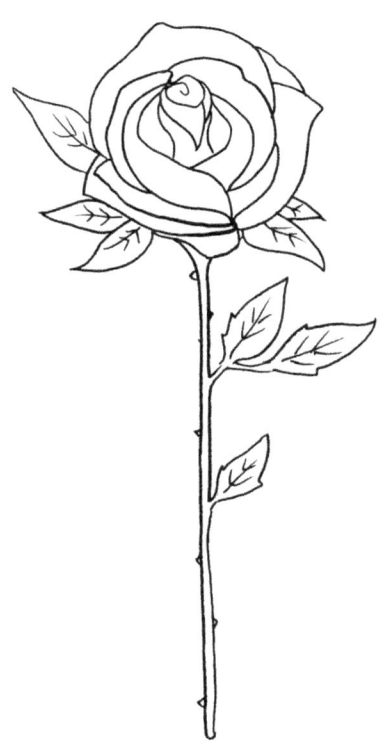

rose

CROSSBOW
rose

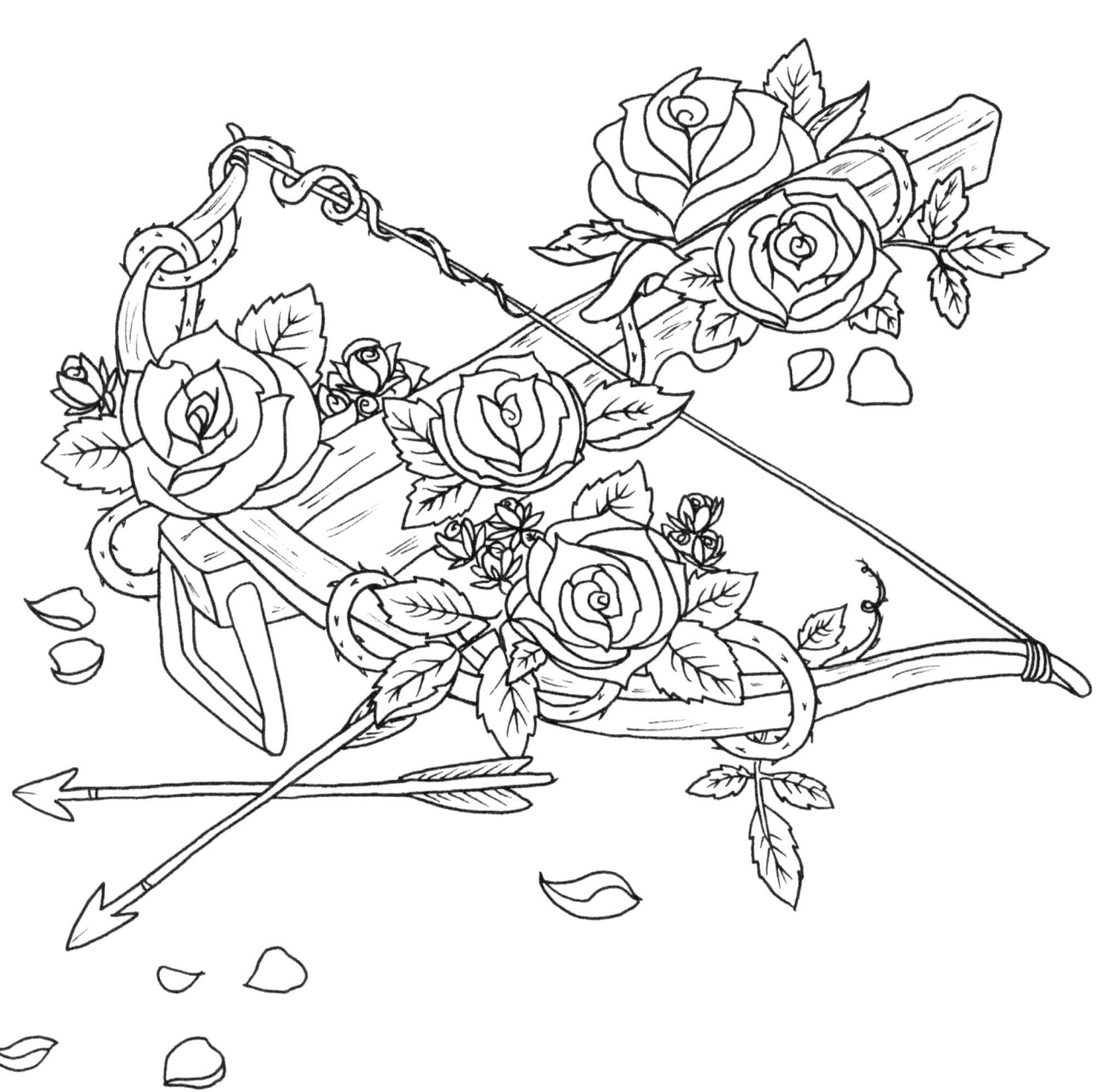

Above the darkened house the night is spread,
The hidden valley holds
Vapour and dew and silence in its folds,
And waters sighing on the river-bed.
No wandering wind there is
To swing the star-wreaths of the clematis
Against the stone;
Out of the hanging woods, above the shores,
One liquid voice of throbbing crystal pours,
Singing alone.

THE BIRD IN THE VALLEY

- VIOLET JACOB -

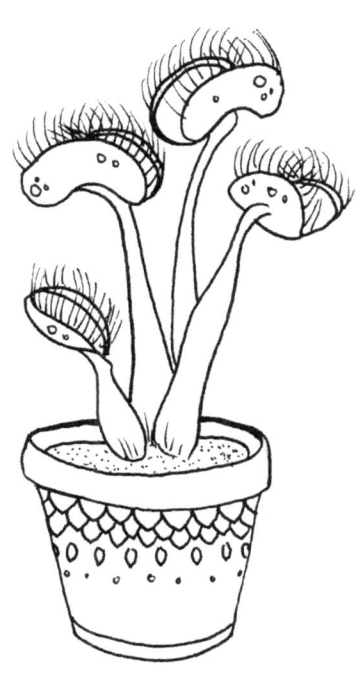

venus fly trap

SCYTHE
wheat - pumpkin - apple - gourd

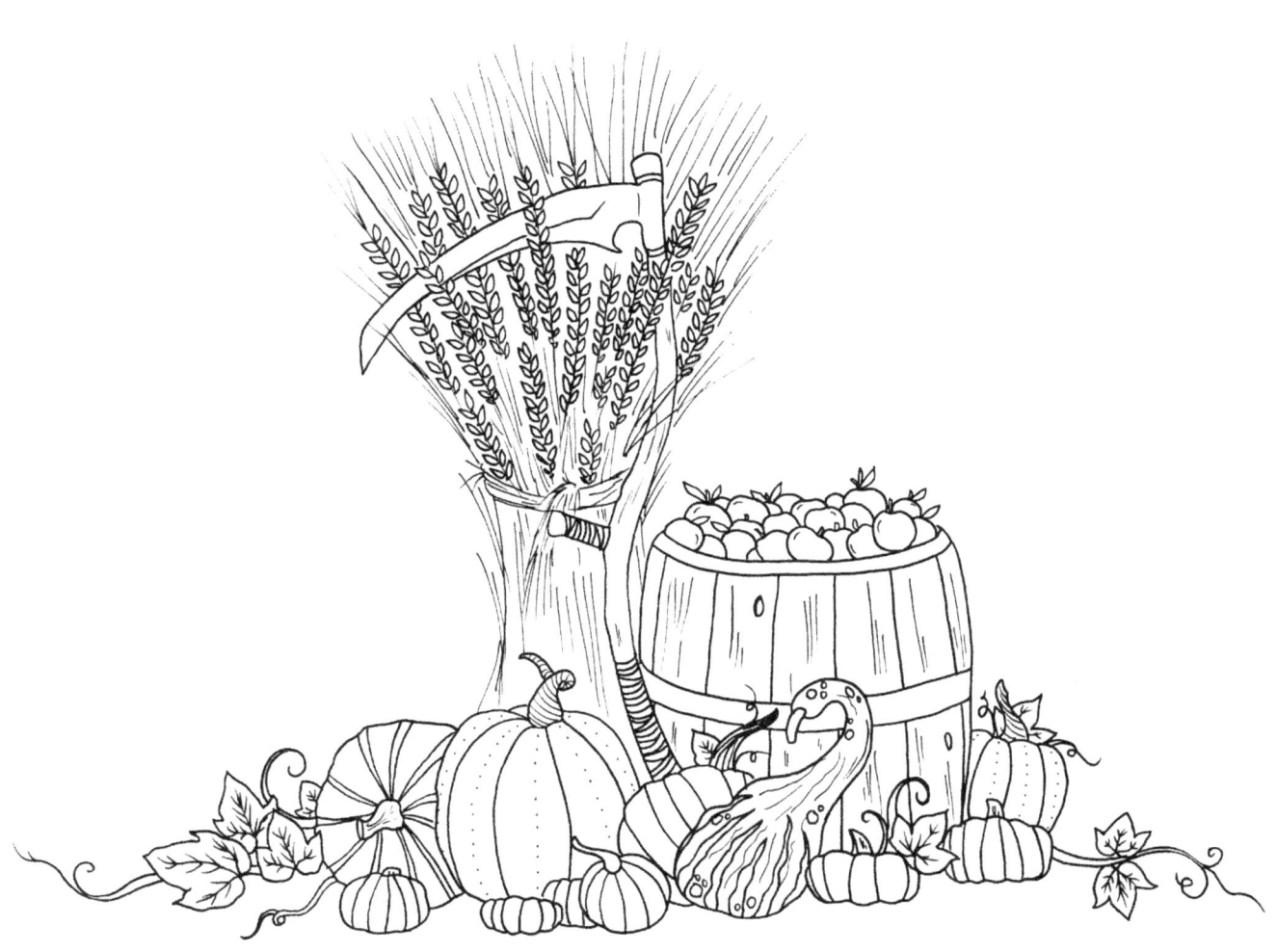

Though Winter frowns to Fancy's raptur'd eyes
The fields may flourish, and gay scenes arise;
The frozen deeps may break their iron bands,
And bid their waters murmur o'er the sands.
Fair Flora may resume her fragrant reign,
And with her flow'ry riches deck the plain;
Sylvanus may diffuse his honours round,
And all the forest may with leaves be crown'd:
Show'rs may descend, and dews their gems disclose,
And nectar sparkle on the blooming rose.

ON IMAGINATION

- PHILLIS WHEATLEY -

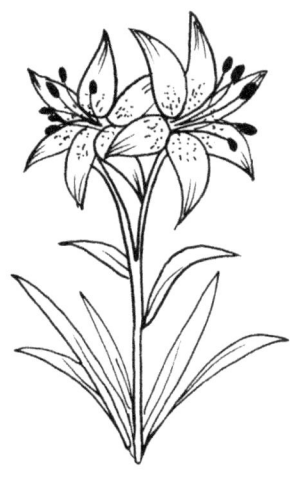

tiger lily

HATCHET
pine - holly - oak

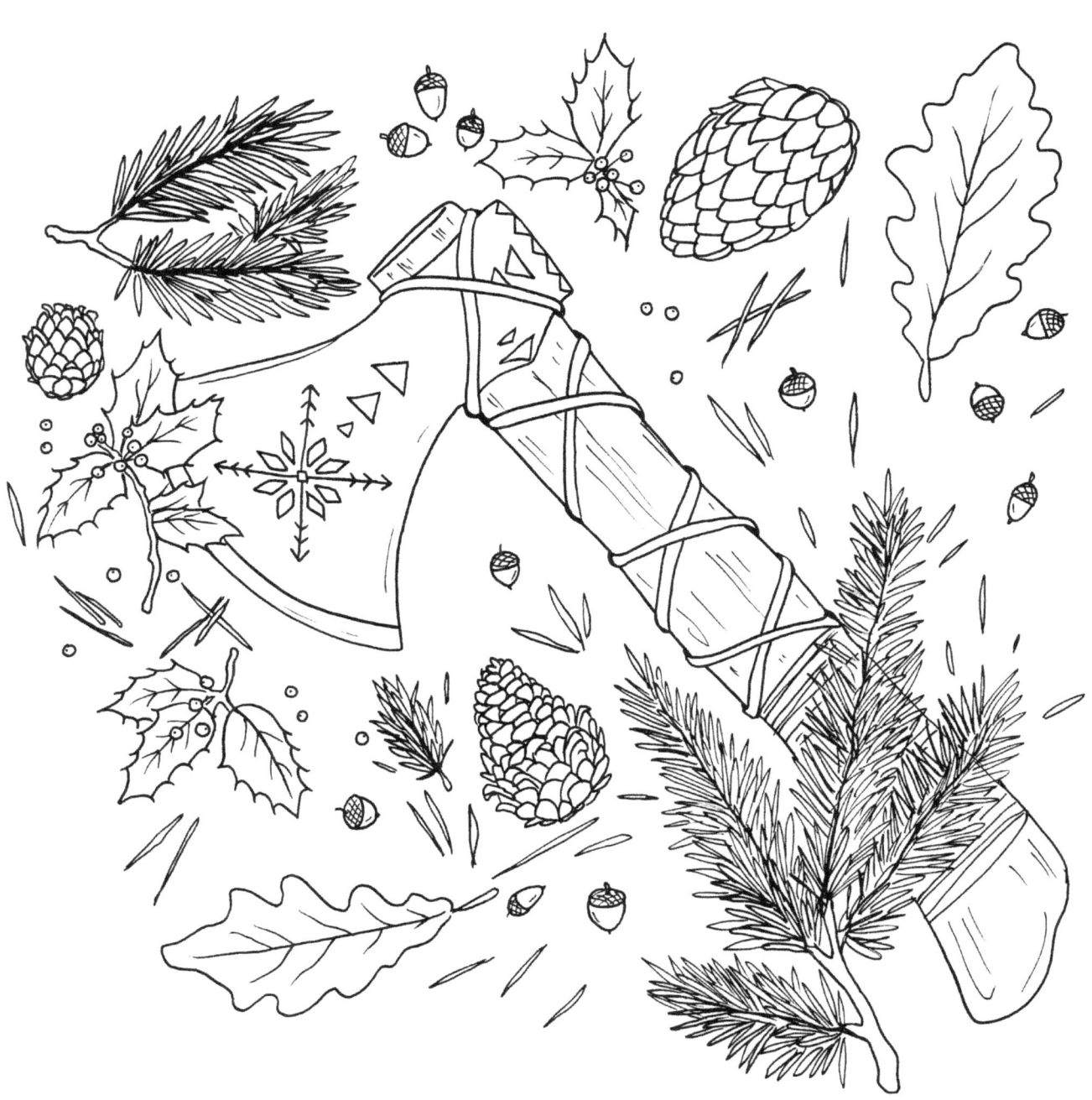

Unfathomable Sea! whose waves are years,
Ocean of Time, whose waters of deep woe
Are brackish with the salt of human tears!
Thou shoreless flood, which in thy ebb and flow
Claspest the limits of mortality!

And sick of prey, yet howling on for more,
Vomitest thy wrecks on its inhospitable shore;
Treacherous in calm, and terrible in storm,
Who shall put forth on thee,
Unfathomable Sea?

TIME

- PERCY BYSSHE SHELLY -

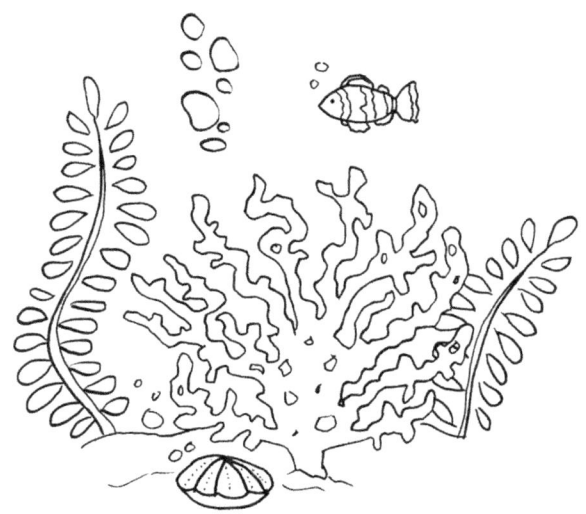

seaweed - coral

TRIDENT
seaweed - barnacles - sea anemone - coral

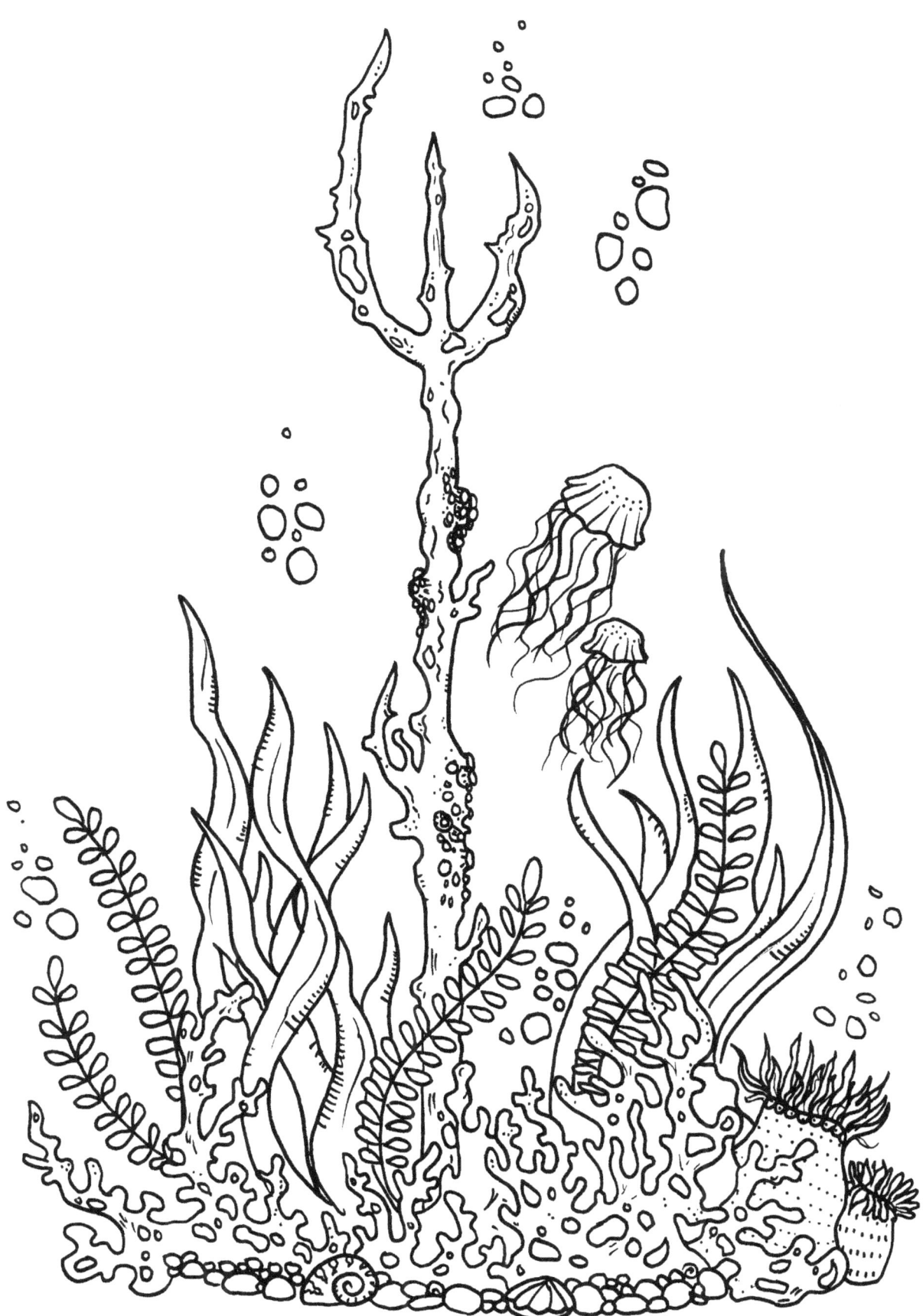

'Fight, gentlemen of England! fight, bold yeomen!
Draw, archers, draw your arrows to the head!
Spur your proud horses hard, and ride in blood;
Amaze the welkin with your broken staves!'

RICHARD III

- WILLIAM SHAKESPEARE -

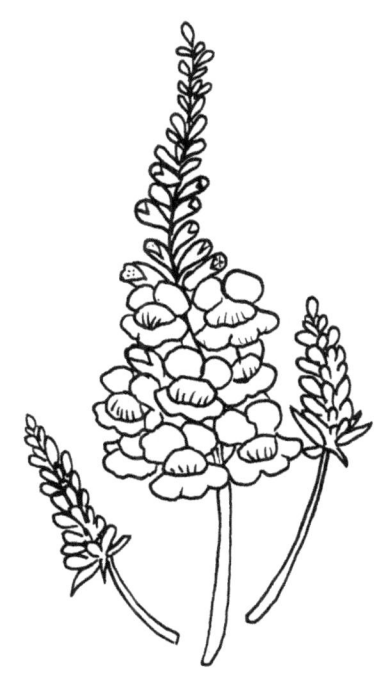

snapdragon

WAR HAMMER
bleeding heart - cranesbill geranium - calendula

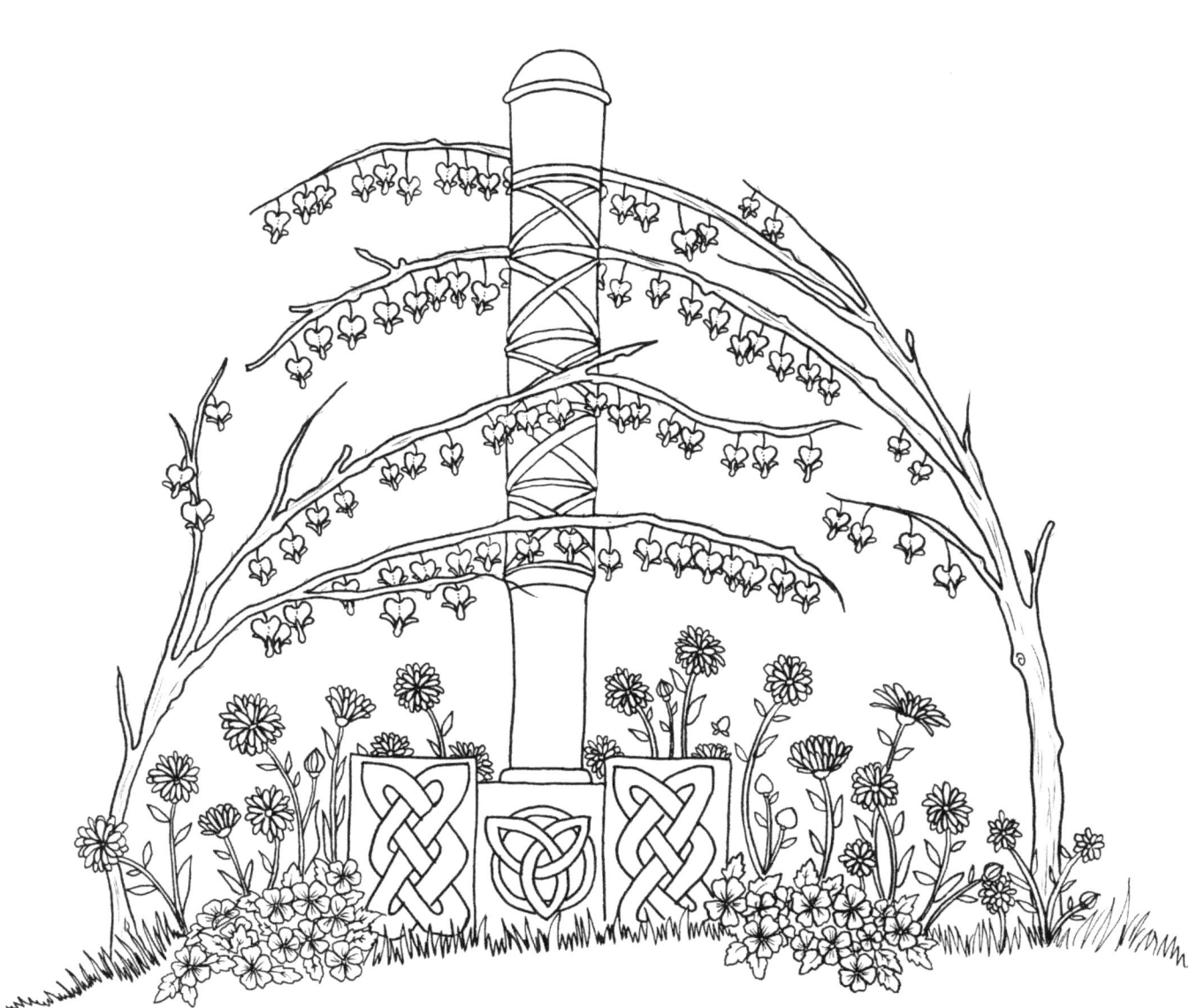

On either side the river lie
Long fields of barley and of rye,
That clothe the wold and meet the sky;
And thro' the field the road runs by
To many-tower'd Camelot;
And up and down the people go,
Gazing where the lilies blow
Round an island there below,
The island of Shalott.

Willows whiten, aspens quiver,
Little breezes dusk and shiver
Thro' the wave that runs for ever
By the island in the river
Flowing down to Camelot.
Four gray walls, and four gray towers,
Overlook a space of flowers,
And the silent isle imbowers
The Lady of Shalott.

THE LADY OF SHALOTT

- ALFRED, LORD TENNYSON -

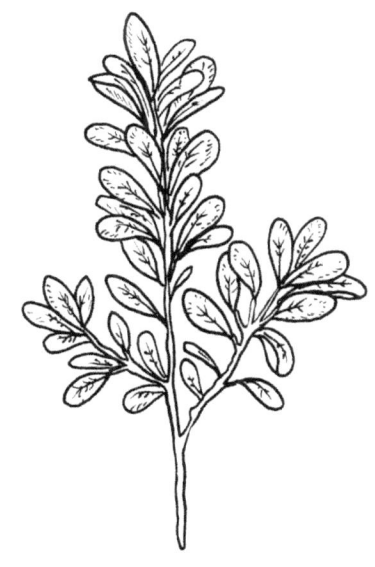

lamb's ear

CLAYMORE
foxglove - thistle - heather - clover

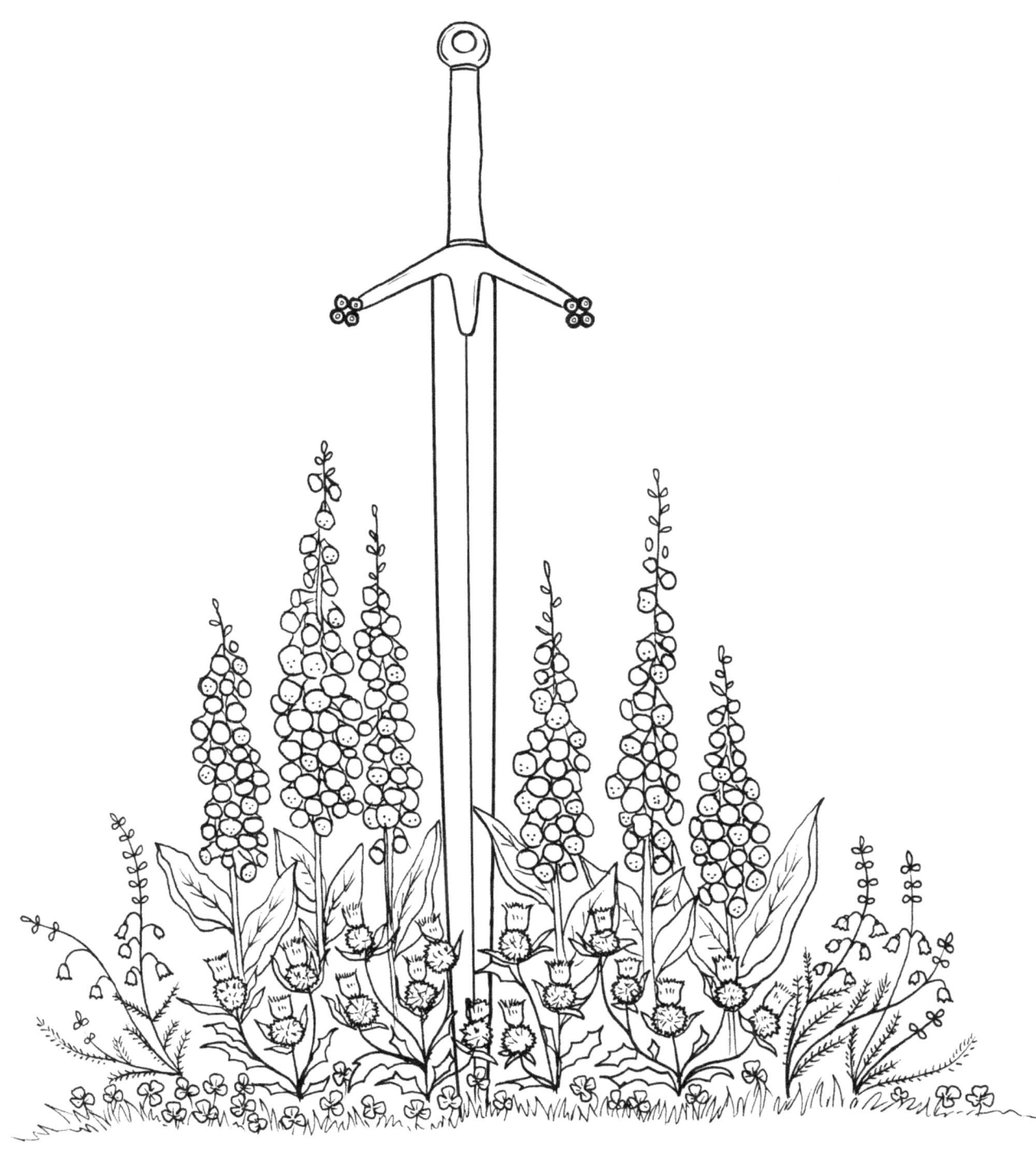

I shot an arrow into the air,
It fell to earth, I knew not where;
For, so swiftly it flew, the sight
Could not follow it in its flight.

I breathed a song into the air,
It fell to earth, I knew not where;
For who has sight so keen and strong,
That it can follow the flight of song?

Long, long afterward, in an oak
I found the arrow, still unbroke;
And the song, from beginning to end,
I found again in the heart of a friend.

THE ARROW AND THE SONG

- HENRY WADSWORTH LONGFELLOW -

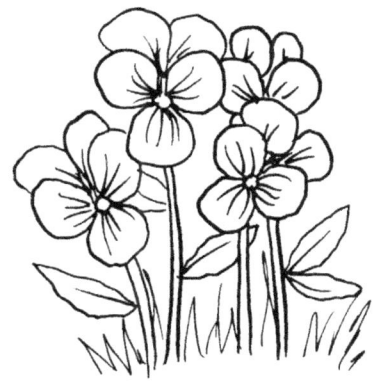

pansy

LONGBOW
forget-me-not - chicory - musk mallow - dog rose

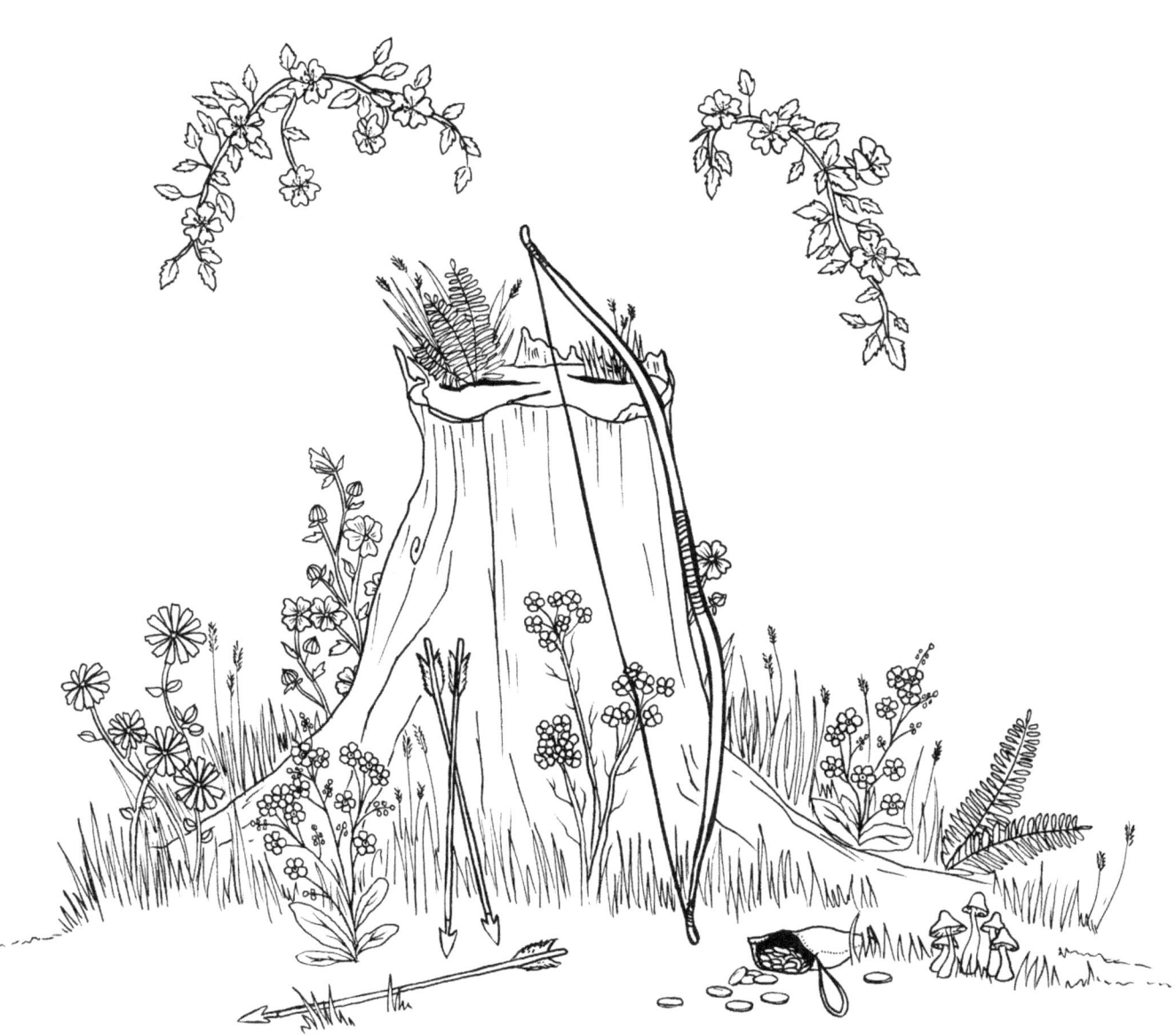

www.ingramcontent.com/pod-product-compliance
Lightning Source LLC
Chambersburg PA
CBHW080622220526

45466CB00010B/3423